Entrepreneurship: MASTERING ABC OF BUSINESS

Aaron Dendero

Text © Aaron Dendero 2013
Illustrations ©Aaron Dendero 2013,
Text and illustrations © revised - 2023

Aaron Dendero has asserted his right to be identified as the author of this work under United Kingdom Copyright, Designs and Patents Act 1988.

All rights reserved. No part of this publication may be reproduced, stored in a retrieval system, or transmitted in any form or by any means, electronic, mechanical, photocopying, recording or otherwise, without the prior permission of the copyright owner.

ISBN-13: 978-1494805418
ISBN-10: 1494805413

DEDICATION

This book is dedicated to my son Alex and daughter Abby.

ACKNOWLEDGMENTS

Every effort has been made to trace all the copyright holders, but if any have been inadvertently overlooked the author will be pleased to make necessary arrangement at the first opportunity.

HOW TO USE THIS BOOK

This tiny book has three distinct parts written straightforwardly all you have to do is to read it part 1 first, followed by part 2 and ultimately part 3.

TABLE OF CONTENTS

PART I:
AN ENTREPRENEUR
The ideas phase

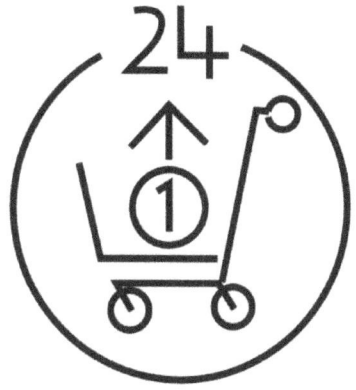

PART II:
AN ENTREPRENEUR DAY-TO-DAY
The starting and day-to-day running phase

PART III:
AN ENTREPRENEUR IN THE LONG TERM
The future and continuity phase

AN ENTREPRENEUR

Who is an entrepreneur?

An entrepreneur is a **profit** motivated one-man band principal seller that has seized and will seize on opportunities to offer for sell repetitively in **added value** in the form of lower prices, customization, improved performance, special features, unforgettable styling, faster service, convenience, higher status, standout packaging and so forth on own or existing product or service using **resources at hand**, to **a market**, day-to-day and in the long term. An entrepreneur can assume identity as a separate entity, this is normally referred to as an enterprise; the formed entity inherits the principal seller's identity. When an entrepreneur scales-up, that is takes a partner, investor, hire people or use third parties, they directly or indirectly contribute towards selling more of the principal seller's product or service.

An entrepreneur day-to-day

How does it all begin, whether be a product or service, it all starts with a prototype, that is, the first example of a product or service from which all later forms are developed, this is achieved by an entrepreneur buying input products and services from other sellers, the common used term for these is suppliers, an entrepreneur will then work around the prototype to the final product or service, once this is done what follows is the determination of who the buyers for the final product or service are, the common used term is customers, then, the means by which an entrepreneur get the final product or service to the customers, commonly known as distribution channels, seldom, an entrepreneur has exclusive access to customers in a market, other sellers to the same customers are the competitors, and while all this is happening, there exists entities that are neither buyers, suppliers, employees or investors, the term used for this is general public.

An entrepreneur in the long term

In the long term, there are conditions beyond an entrepreneur's control that present both opportunities and threats, namely, economic, social, cultural, demographic, natural, technological, political, and legal. Many of one-man band enterprise failures are owners that got completely immersed on day-to-day activities, oblivious of new opportunities and encroaching threats from outside.

Resources at hand

What do brewers, distillers, perfumery and cosmetics enterprises share in common? They are bottlers, the bulk of what they produce is bottled liquids containing alcohol. During the covid pandemic there was a shortage of hand sanitizers, brewers, distillers, perfumery and cosmetics switched production from booze, perfume and cosmetics to producing alcohol hand sanitizers using the same people, raw materials, minor tweaks on equipment and machinery without much new cash injection. This is an example of exploiting opportunities using resources at hand.

RESOURCES

Resources are means to exploit opportunities current and emerging, namely, the money, space, equipment, and people. Profit is made through optimum use of resources.

Money

Money is the government issued real coins and notes in the bank, under a mattress, in a piggy bank or the less versatile peer to peer digital crypto currency. The fact is, whether upfront or on deferred terms, the bulk of payments are still in cash.

Space and equipment

You need space and equipment to do the work - office, basement, garage, workshop, machinery, tools and so forth.

The people

You need people to do the work, even, automation of all things, is initiated and run by people. The key question is who does what?

To understand who does what, we will use the most basic organization structure where jobs are grouped by departments, divided between support and primary activities, these are support activities - Management, HR, finance, legal, Information Technology, procurement, primary activities are inbound logistics, production/processing, outbound logistics, marketing, sales and after sales services.

Management

What has management to do with in an enterprise?

Management has to do with running of an entire enterprise. While there is a requirement for employees to be specialists, the best managers are generalists who understand the pressures of running an enterprise. As a one-man band entrepreneur, you are both a manager and an employee, in your role as a manager, you have to learn to appreciate running a business is complicated, understand the variation in processes that needs action or being left alone, understanding the importance of continuous learning as knowledge does become obsolete and how to motivate yourself internally and externally, thrive to get things done right the first time all the time, allocate your time and prioritize tasks appropriately, delegation, you do not have to do everything yourself, you can assign a portion or the whole of workload to others internally or externally whenever possible. As an enterprise owner, you live and breathe it, employees get compensated in wages, that is their number one priority, their self-interest, make no assumption, they will treat your enterprise as you do, watch your money as you do; you have to find ways to motivate them or else you will end up with backlash or worse a mass departure of people.

Human Resources management

What has Human resources to do with in an enterprise?

Human resources management has to with all matters relating to employment namely recruitment and selection - for hiring, training and development - for equipping, updating, and upgrading knowledge in skills and in turn improve individual productivity, for this to happen there has to be investments, innovation, enterprise and competition, appraisals - for assessing performance, disciplinary and grievances - for maintaining peace and harmony, and rewards - for retention and firing, as demanded by circumstances.

Finance

What has finance to do with in an enterprise? Finance has to do with managing cash in hand and the money that is coming in and going out of an enterprise day to day and in the long term. For cash in hand, Security, access and yield is important, for the whole enterprise, liquidity and profitability are key issues.

Security, access and yield

1. Security is for safety and protection in the bank, your money is safe but not completely protected as if the worst has to happen with your bank there is a maximum you can get from financial compensation schemes.

2. Access with internet and self service banking it is easier to get hold of your cash but there are limits on how much you can withdraw at any one time.

3. Yield how much interest does your money generate.

Liquidity and profitability

Liquidity is the ability to pay debts when they are due on time and profitability is a measure of operating performance. Liquidity is more important than profitability. You can be profitable and still go burst. Profit per unit of sale and trading profit are not the same. The former is the margin added to unit costs the later it total revenues minus total costs of doing business at a given point.

Revenue and expenditure

Money coming in is revenue, money going out is expenditure. Expenditure is further divided into capital and revenue, where capital expenditure has to do with long term investments in real assets namely Property, Plant and Equipment by buying outright, hiring, leasing, or renting, and revenue expenditure has to do with day-to-day investment like purchasing stock, wages, fees, and so forth.

Receipts and payments

The actual cash received on revenues is receipts and the actual cash paid out is payments.

Petty cash

In the past, every other enterprise used to hold a small amount or cash for small purchases and expenses but due to decline in the use of notes and coins, most enterprises hold no cash anymore and instead use business credit cards.

Cash-flow

The difference between money coming in and money going out is crucial. There are two factors that affect cash flow, cash conversion cycle, that is, the number of days it takes to convert stock into cash receipts and frequency of purchase or replacement rate, that is, how often and how long it takes for buyers re-purchase a product or service. Cash-flow can be positive or negative. A negative cash-flow indicates you receive enough cash before you pay out and positive cash-flow is the opposite where you get paid later after you have paid out, a lot of businesses depend on arranged bank overdrafts for this shortfall.

How you can improve cash flow, you can do it in three ways, get paid early, reduce stock holding and negotiate longer deferred terms. That said, it is easier to reduce stock holding as within one's control, getting paid early or longer deferred terms is a mammoth task. If you offer credit to customers, in theory you can charge interest on late payments, but this is easier said than done, negotiating longer credit terms with suppliers isn't easy either.

Wages

The biggest drain to cash flow is wages. Calculating what percentage of an enterprise's incoming cash should go to wages is vital for keeping it afloat. The basic rule based on experience is, in service-based businesses, where no stock is held, payroll can reach the 50% mark without destroying profitability. For a product-based, where stock is held it must be less than 30%.

Enormity vs. duration

There is a tendency among many to people confuse between enormity and duration of a task. On the surface, what might seem as a small task can take the most of person hours to complete whereas a task that seem so big can take the least. One must always do the Maths as person hours are essential for optimum staffing levels and the difference between getting paid for the work done with a profit or doing charity or worse turn into a cowboy - dishonest or careless business person.

Seed capital

Seed capital is the amount needed to start a business. Seldom a start up without any history of trading will be able to raise money either by shares that leads to dilution of ownership or borrowing that leads to interest payments, however it is possible to arrange for an overdraft a short term but normally more expensive form of borrowing depending on creditworthiness.

Legal

What has legal to do with in an enterprise?
Legal has to do with all matters of applicable laws to an enterprise, the bulk of it, is contract law, legally binding implied or written promises by relevant sound mind parties with suppliers, customers, investors, employees, the public and so forth.

Information technology

What has Information Technology to do with in an enterprise?
Information technology has to do with safe and secure handling of information in numerical, text and graphical vector or bitmap format throughout an enterprise using hardware, software, and services.

Procurement

What has procurement to do with in an enterprise?
Procurement has to do with the identification and selection of suppliers and subsequent purchasing activities.

Inbound logistics

What has Inbound logistics to do with in an enterprise?
Inbound logistics has to do with handling and management of stock coming into an enterprise, unloading, inspection, booking in, stock receipts, counting, stock preparation, storage and issuing to production for Just-In-Time systems are typical activities.

Production

What has production to do with in an enterprise?
Production has to do with the process of making of new products, assembling orders or providing a service. Activities involved are scheduling, order downloads, order picking on manual or automated systems, serving and so forth.
Note: **Research and development (R&D)** is part of production, creating and playing around with prototypes.

Outbound logistics

What has outbound logistics to do with in an enterprise? Outbound logistics has to do with handling and management of stock going out to customers, activities involved are, picking, packing into units of dispatch or unit loading devices consolidation, labelling, loading, transportation and so forth.

Marketing

What has Marketing to do with in an enterprise? Marketing has to do with acquisition of new customers by pre-selling a product or service through blending Product, Placement, Promotion, People, Processes, Physical evidence and Pricing (7Ps) elements into a Unique Selling Proposition that will induce buyers into trying a product or service and repeat the message for the existing for a repeat purchase. A seller sells features a buyer buys benefits.

Pricing

Pricing makes or breaks sales. The trick here is to identify all the costs involved in production, placement, promotion, people involved for a product and for a service additional processes and then determine the optimum price bearing in mind what people pay for similar products or services in the market.

Example

Products normally come as standalone, that is complete on their own or base and complementary. To price a standalone, you can identify costs as above and add a percentage margin, say 5, 10 percent and so forth, for the base and complementary, you can price a base at lower price to allow entry and higher on complementary to compensate of what you have lost on the base, printer vs. toners/cartridges, and the opposite, pricing the base higher to restrict entry and complementary lower, golf club green fees vs. golf equipment. You can do price discrimination, little to do with costs, by time, location, use type and so forth.

Sales

What has sales to do with in an enterprise? Sales have to do with customers' interaction and persuasion, the aim is to provide customers with all the necessary information needed for buying decision, face to face, self-service or remotely using sales literature, product demonstrations, or sales aids.

After-sales services

What has after-sales to do with in an enterprise? After sales services have to do with customer retention, one cannot underestimate the importance of repeat customers, activities involved are installations, upgrades, troubleshooting, exchanges, warranties, returns, safe disposal and so forth, dealt with face to face or remotely.

MARKET

What is a market?

A **market** is physical or non-physical place where sellers, offer **products** or **services** at the **price** and **quantities** buyers are willing and able to pay using their **incomes**.

PRODUCT

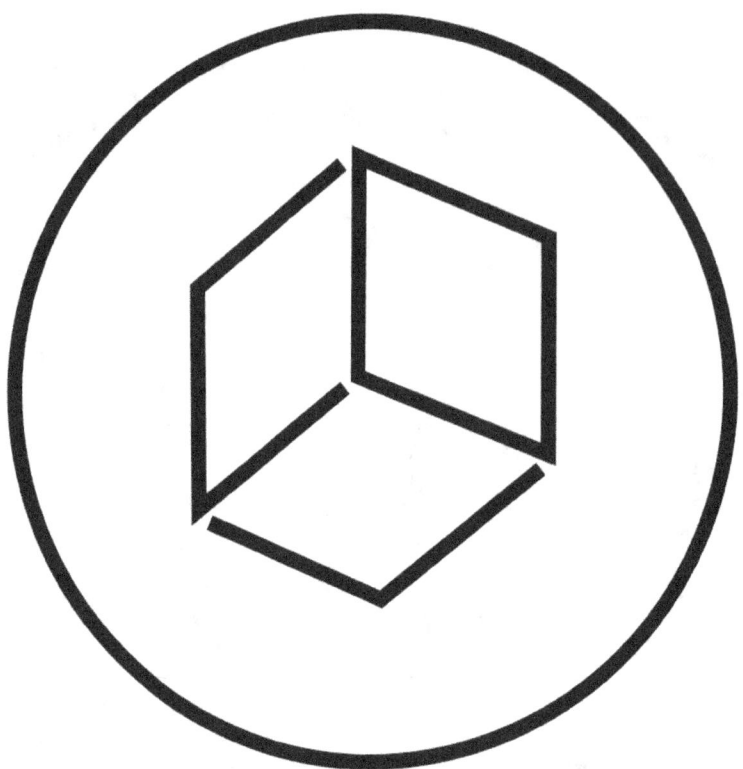

What is a product?

A product is any 3 dimensional physical thing, that is, has length, width and depth or thickness that you can touch, feel or hold which once sold and fully paid for results in transfer of ownership from a seller to a buyer. Every single product that is offered for sell as at or after market is human harvested, extracted, or made by hand or machine. At every stage effort is applied and **value is added**, costs are incurred, and passed to the customers in prices charged accordingly. Every product on offer has a limited useful life that could be in seconds, minutes, hours, days, years, decades, centuries and who knows may be millennium. Long-life product is one that is intended to be used repeatedly over a long period of time and thus doesn't need to be purchased and restocked frequently, short life product is one that is intended to be used once or repeatedly over a short period of time and thus does need to be purchased and restocked frequently.

Significant value addition

Significant value addition is the **noticeable added value** that the **buyer** is willing and able to **pay for**.

Example:
Cars do come with standard and optional features, you can buy of the forecourt as it is or customize it by adding different colour, wheels, interior trim, tow-bar, spoiler and so forth.

Significant product value addition

Example 1
Human harvested value addition
Untreated timber also known as sawn timber is timber in its natural state and thus offers no protection to environmental conditions and is cheaper whereas the pressure impregnated treated timber is expensive as it has a protection for longer lifespan. Pressure impregnation is the added value.

Example 2
Human extracted value addition
A barrel of crude petroleum is cheaper than of a refined, refinery is the added value.

Example 3
Human made value addition
A single glazed glass pane is cheaper than a double glazed, glazing is value added.
There are countless examples I can give but the one above, are enough to get the point.

SERVICE

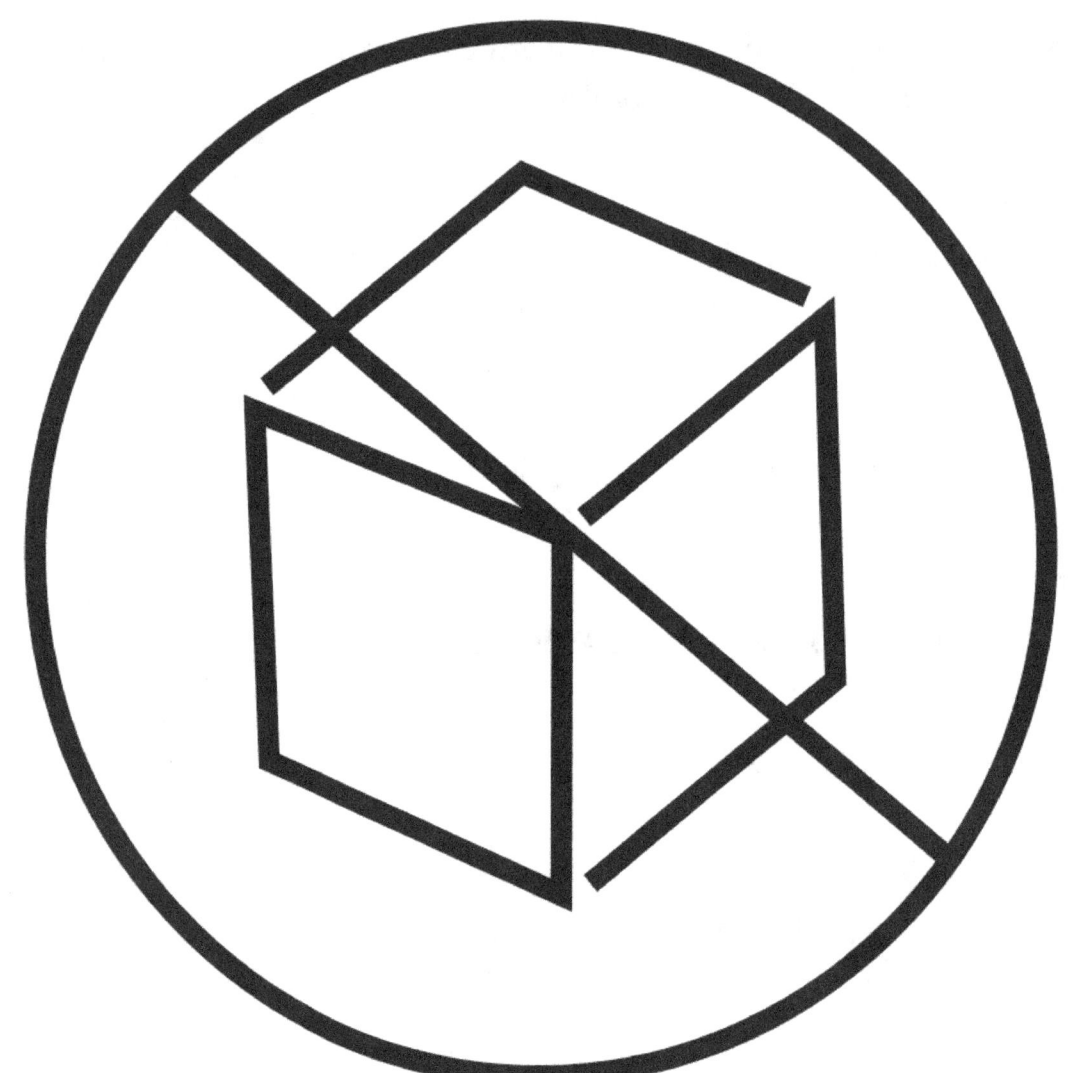

What is a service?

A service is the non-physical product equivalent, which once sold and fully paid for does not result in transfer of ownership from a seller to a buyer. Every service that is offered for sell requires human effort. The applied effort in knowledge and skills is the added value. A provided service cannot be restocked but can be purchased upfront or on subscription and used once or repeatedly over a short or long period of time.

Significant service value addition

Example 1:

Say you go to a dentist for dental implant, the implanting that requires high level of skills and expertise is the added significant value addition.

Example 2:

Say you go to a DIY store, most paints come with off the shelf standard colours, yet there is a paint mixing service for any colour of your choosing, the paint mixing technology, operator's skills and expertise are the significant value additions.

Example 3:

Say you bought a commercial oven, installation requires high level of skills and expertise and safe disposal requires manpower and transportation, installation and safe disposal are significant value additions.

Aftermarket

Aftermarket is the market for follow on complementary products for aesthetic, enhancement, maintenance, or repair purposes of the previous bought base product. After market products are sold as used, reconditioned, restored, refurbished, or brand-new.

Examples of aftermarket product and services :

Printer toners and cartridges, software upgrades, modifications, customizations, restorations, interim, full and major car services and so forth.

FACT:

Automotive aftermarket, that is the market involved with manufacturing, remanufacturing, distribution, retailing, and installation of all complementary vehicle parts, chemicals, equipment, lubricants, and accessories is one of the biggest, it supports hundreds of thousands of jobs and bringing in billions of pounds to the UK economy.

PRICE

Price is value equivalent of a product or service.

QUANTITY

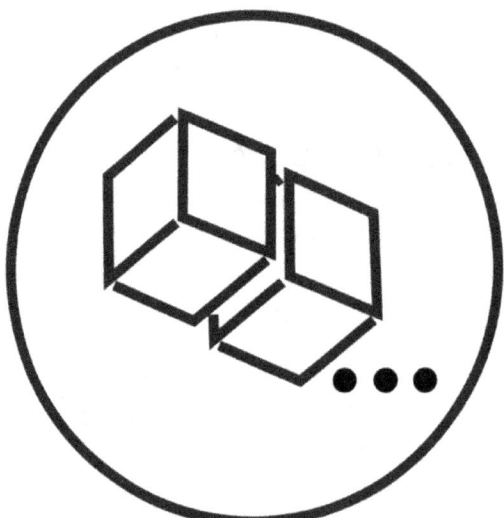

Quantity is the amount of products offered for sell. A service is qualitative and per se unquantifiable.

INCOME

Income is the money available to buy products or services on offer.

Buyers spending

Buyers normally divide their spending from their incomes into two categories:

Essential purchases

Essential purchases involve shopping for a wide range of everyday goods for personal use or consumption and enterprises use.
Essential enterprises includes supermarkets, pharmacies, off-licences, petrol stations, newsagents, home and hardware stores, hauliers, garages and so forth

Discretionary purchases

Discretionary purchases involve shopping for non everyday goods for whatever intended use which can be postponed or cancelled all together.

Non-essential enterprises are all the others.

HOW IMPORTANT IS CREDIT?

SOURCE: BANK OF ENGLAND (BOE), ONS, FLA

CREDIT IS BIG BUSINESS!

Access to credit is income. The more creditworthy, the more and at lower interest both enterprises and individuals borrow money.

FIGURES:

According to Bank of England, the average UK consumers (households) debt (excluding student loans) is equivalent to around 123% of total household income, of this, mortgage debt accounts for around 80 percent of credit. According to Finance and Leasing Association (FLA), over 86.5 percent of new private cars are bought by consumers using finance supplied by its members annually. The government and enterprises are no way better, according to Office of National Statistics (ONS) UK general government gross debt was £2,223.0 billion at the end of the financial year ending March 2021, equivalent to 103.6% of gross domestic product (GDP), according to BoE Aggregate corporate debt was £1.4 trillion between end of 2019 and 2021 Q1 that equates to average corporate debt-to-earnings ratio of 349%.

Correlation among price, quantity, and income

Price, quantity, and income affect demand and supply of products or services, that is how many of products or how much of services is wanted in a market, there are products or services whose demand rise as income rises, for example groccries, when income rises, people switch from pen eggs to free range, when it rises further from free range to organic, in travel, most people travel economy class, once their income rises, they upgrade to business class and when the income rises further, they go first class, there are some products whose demand rises as income falls, take for example branded, supermarket own brand and generic groceries, when income falls people switch from branded to supermarket own brands, when income falls further, they switch from supermarket own brands to generic, the name used by supermarket for these products is essentials, in travel, when income falls first class travel is downgraded to business and if it falls further to economy, there are some products and services whose demand stay the same regardless of income rise or fall, for example staple foods, the type of food that is consumed most in a country namely wheat, rice, corn, potatoes and so forth, there are rare things whose demand rises as income rises above a certain threshold, that is, people become rich, like collector items in arts, vehicles, luxury products like diamonds, high performance cars and so forth.

Want

Unlike needs that are finite, we all need clothing, food, shelter, healthcare, and so forth, Wants are infinite and is what drive capitalist, free market, free enterprise system, people with capital have the power to invest as they please, people with money to spend on products or services, have the power to choose and buy what they want, from anywhere as they see fit.

Price sensitivity

Buyers are price sensitive. The way most seller's work around this problem is size, weight, ingredients reduction at the same price. Say for example, a 100grams bar of chocolate is sold for a pound, the main ingredient is cocoa, if the price of cocoa increases rather than increasing the price, the producer, reduce a few grams in a bar and keep price the same.

Preference

There is also a question of personal preference; income does affect preference in most instances. Surely you would trade sardines for shrimps, if you can afford or if you live in a shack and suddenly you have enough money to afford a mansion, you'd buy one, if you had a boat, you'd upgrade to a yacht.

Capacity

At any one time, sellers some more than others tend to have maximum amount of products they can produce or limited service they can provide, this is fixed capacity. Stadiums, arenas, air, water, and land transport vehicles to name but a few, all of these have fixed capacity, in space, the people, tools, equipment and machinery to do the job. To utilize capacity fully and make money, sellers use ranking to charge different prices. Say for example First class flight is around two times business class, business class is around 4 times economy class, meaning, every 1 first class passenger pays for 2 business class or 8 economy passengers, 1 business class passenger pays for 4 economy class passengers. For non no frills, scheduled flight airlines first and business class are the most profitable.

Product vs. service-based enterprise

A product-based enterprise at or after market turns over stock to generate revenues, a service based-enterprises, turns-over knowledge and skills to generate revenues; they both incur costs in the process. Revenues less costs equal profit, revenues equal costs, neither profit nor loss, revenues more costs equal loss.

Business model
Business model is an enterprise's long-term plan on how it is going to make money from its products or services. Understanding how individuals and industry are funded or financed is very important.

Example 1:
Say you are running a tourist souvenir shop that relies heavily on footfall, that is the number of tourists coming to your shop and spend mostly their hard earned cash in wages, if tourism slows down or footfall drops, you have to review your business model.

Example 2:
Say you are running a pharmaceutical research and development enterprise, most of the funding is coming from a mix of government in grants, subsidies, tax credits and financing is from well-off investors, investment banks, and other financial institutions.
If there are any significant changes from either of the sources, you have to review your business model.

Example 3:
Say you are a property developer, majority of people will need mortgages to buy property, if the mortgage market changes significantly, you have to review your business model.

PART II:

An entrepreneur day to day

AN ENTERPRISE'S SUPPLIERS

Suppliers are sellers that provide an enterprise with ingredients in the form of products and services required to produce its products or provide services. Suppliers are essential to every enterprise's success.

Importance of suppliers
Source: airbus.com

Around 80% of Airbus' activity is sourced, that is, contracted to outside suppliers. Airbus works with more than 12,000 suppliers worldwide that provide products and services for flying, that is, direct procurement and indirect procurement of non-flying parts, from aero structures, equipment and systems, material and parts, propulsion, cabin procurement to specialised IT and services with an average annual spend of approximately €49.6 billion.

Number, size, and strength of suppliers

The smaller the number, the larger and the bigger the buying power the less the bargaining power for the smaller buyer.

Product rules of origin

Product rules of origin refers to the last country where significant manufacturing process was carried out, where within the EU for tariff free purposes, an EU exporter must demonstrate that over 55 per cent of the value of the product value was created within the EU, if suppliers pay tariff, they won't absorb the cost rather they will pass it to you. This will also impact, you if you use these as inputs to produce other products when it comes to exporting.

Lead times

Lead time is the duration between placing an order or application and receiving it or getting the go ahead. Suppliers do have their own specified lead times, at times, they can make an exception for an extra amount and expedite but one must use this in exceptional circumstances only as is very expensive. The basic rule based on experience is, apart from essential items that are used daily, if there exists same or next day delivery and availability is reliable, whenever possible order for items to be delivered nearest to the time they will be needed and thus avoid holding stock. Lead times are not exclusive to products, they also apply to services. In heavily regulated industries, every project must be approved, and proper documentation issued before it can commence.

Example of lead times

Say you are a property developer, almost every project does need planning permission or if your enterprise does drug development, you need approvals before any study can commence, if your enterprise goods, must go through customs clearance, there might be considerable delays, these are just few examples, you must take into considerations.

Minimum quantities

Suppliers do implement minimum quantities or value. The bigger the supplier the higher the threshold, in certain situations, if what one wants to buy falls below the threshold, big suppliers will direct you to distributors or agents where often you pay more than you would have if you ordered directly, there is a way to get around this using, pooling, that is, joining forces with others and buy together in bulk. If you do not have a choice, you can buy the minimum quantity and add it to the price you charge the customers to compensate for wastages rather than absorbing costs.

Request for quotation RFQ

Ideally, before you place any first order you should request a quotation from a few suppliers so you can compare prices and understand their terms and conditions. You should keep tabs and review at least annually as most suppliers tend to change their prices around the same time.

Supplier evaluation and selection

Once you have responses on your RFQs, you review and select suppliers that offer you the best of terms and after, if possible, apply for credit account accordingly.

Standard vs custom made

Ideally, you should stick to standard products wherever possible, as customization is a specification that is, own written instructions on the product or service requirements that takes time and costs more money. You should keep variety to a minimum.

Delivery

There tend to be a limit by geography, weight, size, value on so forth, and minimum spend from most suppliers, wherever possible you should look at avoiding or minimizing delivery charges by taken aforementioned factors into account, say for example if geography is a factor, try as much as you can to find local suppliers, if is value and is not urgent, wait until you can consolidate orders to a minimum value and qualify for free delivery and so forth.

Supply vulnerabilities

Due to long and complex global supply, from the point of origin, production to consumption and reversal back to the point of production for recapturing value as in recycling or safe disposal, there is always a risk to supplies somewhere, somehow that may affect your enterprise day to day operations and in the long run. Quality is always an issue as is interpreted differently across the world, there is a compliance issue, matters of the law, every country has its own laws, enterprises can be sanctioned, expelled, lose licenses, and so forth. The point here is, whatever you order, you must assess the vulnerabilities and order from safe places where there is parity in quality and law from your country of operation or implement system that will ensure all these requirements are met.

Dangers of relying on one supplier

The basic rule based on experience is, unless there is only one supplier, you should never allow more than a third of your supplies to come from one supplier as if it happens to lose that supplier and there is no other available to plug the gap, a third of your supplies is gone, you will be in trouble.

Example: Lesson from British Airways

> In 2005 over 110,000 British Airways (BA) passengers were stranded at Heathrow Airport due to an unofficial strike by catering staff at Gate Gourmet. What happened to British Airways was not only a public-relations disaster but also losses that reached tens of millions of pounds. Reason for this chaos was Gate Gourmet was BA only supplier for their in-flight meals at Heathrow.

Dangers of relying on big suppliers

Large suppliers shift high volumes, they do prioritize distribution channels capable of helping them achieve their sales volume at the expense the smaller ones that won't.

Example: Lesson from small independents

> The sportswear enterprises, Adidas, ASICS and Nike, they all stopped supplying their products to small independent retailers and focus instead on larger chains and direct to consumer (DTC) online sales, and in a flash those small independent retailers went out of business.

AN ENTERPRISE'S CUSTOMERS

An enterprise can sell exclusively to individuals for personal use by targeting specific groups based on where they live, how they behave, how they think, their ages, gender, ethnicity, education, income, marriage and so forth or to other enterprises for conversion, consumption, or resale.

If an enterprise sells exclusively to individuals the common term for it is Business to Consumer abbreviated B2B, if an enterprise sells exclusively to other enterprises the common term for it is Business to Business abbreviated B2B, an enterprise can be both a B2C and B2B.

The most important customer is the repeat rather than the one-off.

Importance of repeat customers
A lesson from Activision Blizzard Guitar Hero, P&G Gillette and mobile phone enterprises.

Guitar Hero was once a hot property in every teenager's room, but the owner Activision Blizzard, disbanded it due to falling sales, despite many reasons the company explained like expensive copyright fees, manufacturing costs, the main reason for the demise was, Guitar Hero was a packaged non-disposable starter bundle, a guitar and a disc, a one off purchase.

Gillette's starter bundle comes with razor handle and razor blades, whereas razor handles are non-disposable and blades are and thus blades that have to be replenished frequently, if it was not for blades Gillette would have been another Guitar hero.

Cellular starter bundle comes with a handset, SIM card and credit, whereas Handset and SIM are non-disposable, credit by subscriptions with contract or pay as you go, is disposable, if it wasn't for subscribers repeat credit purchases, they too would have faced the same fate as Guitar hero.

Switching

Statistically, over 98% of customers don't switch banks, 100% don't switch water and sewerage as suppliers have a regional monopoly, the same apply to gas and electricity, insurance, most customers don't switch supermarkets due to convenience as local planning permissions does disperse them geographically, even when click and collect or delivery the trend is the same and so forth.
REPEAT CUSTOMERS BY DEFAULT! Won customers without constantly competing for!

Selling to individuals vs. enterprises

The difference between selling to individuals for personal use and enterprises is, individuals tend to pay upfront or on take it or leave it credit terms as offered by the seller in own or brokers' capacity, and enterprise mostly pay on deferred terms as per trade credit agreement, except when is a one-off purchase, where they will pay on a pro-forma invoice - pay upfront for products or services before they are supplied.

When selling to individuals, with exception of things like souvenirs, art and crafts and similar sorts, hardly anyone haggles for a pair of trouser or shoes in the shop, but enterprises rarely do so unless is small purchases. There is also forward purchase, most common in oil and energy market, where enterprises especially the large ones can buy at a fixed (hedged) price now for a specific period in a future, where if prices rise it is their gain, if it falls, is their loss.

Competitive tendering

A common process for awarding government contracts to private enterprises. Most not if all opportunities to supply products or services to the public sector are done through competitive tendering. The cheapest bidder used to be the criteria but after many failures the UK government has adopted a Most Economically advantageous tendering, that is, tendering that gives the best value for money. There is also a value approach where any project under a certain value is only open to SMEs small and medium enterprises only. Private enterprises also use tendering in purchasing some services, like cleaning, facilities management and so forth.

Spending power

The bigger the customer the more bargaining power, for a B2C, the more spending powers individuals have, the pickier they are, for a B2B, the more spending power of the customer, the more the discount expectation.

Trends or fads vs classic or standard items

Most of the products consumed or services provided will either be standard, that is, stays as they are, or fad that comes and go. There tend to be a hype around trendy items that fades away rather quickly where the standard items endure the test of time unchanged. For example, only recently, there was a huge rise in meat free (vegan) products demand and suddenly demand has vanished. The humble classic blue denim jeans never run out of fashion.

Dangers of relying on one customer

There is a tendency of micro and small enterprises to rely heavily on one customer, this is a trap, it is living dangerously, the basic rule based on experience is, you should never allow more than a third of your sales to come from one customer as if it happens to lose that customer and there is no other available to plug the gap, a third of your business is gone, you will be lucky to survive.

Dangers of relying on one customer

Example: Lesson from BAE Systems

> In 2009 (British Aerospace Engineering) BAE Systems, Europe's biggest defence company whose fortune depends on **conflict**, full-year profit rose 94pc after wars in Iraq and Afghanistan spurred demand for its armoured vehicles, bomb-disposal robots and bullet-proof vests, then suddenly 2013 there is no conflict hence no demand, it closed its shipyard at Portsmouth as there would no longer be enough orders to sustain the site. The reason is simple; the site depended entirely on one customer – The Ministry of Defence (MoD) contract.

AN ENTERPRISE'S DISTRIBUTION CHANNELS

Distribution channels are physical or non-physical outlets an enterprise uses to get products or provide services to the customers.

Figures:

Even with online shopping, 97% of products are still sold through intermediaries, namely distributors, wholesalers, retailers, and agents. Meaning, only 3% of products are sold directly from producers.

Types of intermediaries

1. A distributor (dealer, re-seller) is an enterprise that buys products in large quantities at a discount from producers and re-sells them again to other enterprises or individuals.

2. A wholesaler is an enterprise that buys products in large quantities at a discount from normally from distributors and re-sells them again to other enterprises, typically retailers.

3. A retailer is an enterprise that makes own products or buys products in large quantities at a discount from distributors, and re-sell them to individuals singly or in relatively small quantities for personal use.

4. An agent is paid commission as a percentage of selling price as in accordance with the sale conditions and the agent agreement with the producers.

Advantages of marketing intermediaries

Example

> Levi Roots, prior to appearing on Dragons Den, his **reggae-reggae sauce** was only available on his website or at the annual Notting - Hill Carnival. As soon as he secured the backing of Dragons' Den judges Peter Jones and Richard Farleigh in 2007, his reggae-reggae sauce went on sale in 600 Sainsbury's stores. From a single direct channel to an intermediary with 600 outlets, that is a mammoth leap, the rest is history.

Drawbacks of marketing intermediaries

In 2015 Tesco pulled Schweppes from it stores shelves due to price rise dispute with Coca-Cola. In 2016 Tesco removed Unilever products from its e-commerce website due to a dispute with Unilever over price rises. All these disputes were short lived as TESCO, UK giant backed down and re-instated the products due to customer complaints, the two global giants Coca-Cola and Unilever were unscathed, however, if it was a small enterprise the consequences could have been severe.

Modes of distribution and transportation

Size, value, volume, geographical location will determine modes of distribution and transportation respectively. There are three modes of distribution you can use, that is, indiscriminately to all outlets, by discrimination to many or discrimination to a few outlets. As for transportation, it can be water, air or land or a combination using general or specialist vehicles.

Over two-thirds of products are transported from the point of production to the point of consumption and reverse for recycling or safe disposal via third party, meaning, only a third of producers use own transport. Having own fleet and storage and distribution facilities require huge upfront investment,

It makes a lot of sense to outsource as third party logistics (3PL) companies have resources and are better equipped to deal with all types of products shipments on land, water and air across the globe.

Third party logistics big players

Some of the biggest 3PL enterprises in the world: Kuehne+Nagel, DHL Supply Chain and Global forwarding, DSV, DB Schenker, to name but a few.

AN ENTERPRISE'S COMPETITORS

Competitors are rival enterprises that an enterprise shares the customers with by offering a category of products or services with common characteristics. Competition determines whether a market is profitable and what it takes to enter. In the beginning and the long term an enterprise can compete on either price or differentiation, where, price competition is achieved through low costs normally to a wider market, differentiation is achieved through noticeable difference to the wider or narrow market.

Identifying a competitor - example 1

Sector of industry	Industry	Product	Function	Enterprises	Market segment	Common characteristics
Primary	Agriculture	Farm machinery	Harvesting	Kubota Claas	Combine harvesters	Shakers
						Rotors
						Hybrids

Shakers, rotors and Hybrids are individual common characteristics, competition is between Kubota's shaker and Claas shaker, Kubota's Rotor and Claas Rotor, Kubota's hybrid and Claas Hybrid not Kubota and Claas.

Identifying a competitor - example 2

Sector of industry	Industry	Product	Function	Enterprises	Market segment	Common characteristics
Secondary	Automobile	Luxury cars	Transportation	Audi, BMW, Lexus, Mercedes	entry level luxury	four-door saloon
						BMW 3 Series, Lexus IS, Audi A4, Mercedes-Benz-C-Class
					mid luxury	Mercedes Benz-E-Class, BMW 5 Series, Audi A6, Lexus ES
					high end luxury	Mercedes Benz-S-Class, BMW 7 Series, Audi A8, Lexus LS

Four door saloons is the common characteristic, It is not a four way competition – Audi vs. BMW vs. Mercedes vs. Lexus but their respective entry, mid or high luxury level vehicles. So BMW 3 Series does compete with Lexus IS, Audi A4, and Mercedes-Benz-C-Class at entry level four door saloon and so forth.

Identifying a competitor - services

Sector of industry	Industry	Service	Function	Market	Market segment	Enterprises	Common characteristics
Tertiary	Leisure	Football	Entertainment	Men English football league 2023/24 Season	Premier League	Arsenal Aston Villa Brentford Brighton and Hove Albion Bournemouth Burnley Chelsea Crystal Palace Everton Fulham Liverpool Luton Town Manchester City Manchester United Newcastle United Nottingham Forest Sheffield United Tottenham Hotspur West Ham United Wolverhampton Wanderers	Full-time professional

Common characteristics of the Premier league is all the players in all the teams are full-time professional footballers. The ultimate goal for the 20 competing clubs is to be crowned premier league champions and all the perks that come with winning it and secondly not to be relegated and go down with the costs that come with demotion to the lower English football league tiers.

Market and competition characteristics

1. If the market has many but small competitors that offer the same products or services, the market is easier to enter but less profitable. Enterprises dealing with fresh produce in local markets are an example of this.

2. If the market has many but small competitors that offer different products or services, the market is easier to enter, and is profitable. Enterprises dealing in arts and crafts in physical or online shops are an example of this.

3. If the market has a few but big competitors that offer the same or similar products or services, the market is profitable but difficult to enter. Premier league clubs, mobile telephone networks, banks, supermarkets, digital platforms are examples.

4. If the market has no competitors, it's profitable but impossible to enter as only governments do allow for such an enterprise to exist. Regional water supplies, National grid, Network rail are examples.

Competitive advantage

Significant product or knowhow differentiation that is legally or proprietary protected is an enterprise's competitive advantage.

Price or differentiation

If price is a factor and low costs cannot be achieved or if differentiation is a factor and noticeable difference cannot be achieved, there is no point to enter either of the market.
If price competition is the chosen route and along the way low costs can no longer be achieved or differentiation is the chosen route and along the way it can no longer be achieved, it is time for an enterprise to cut its losses and exit.

THE GENERAL PUBLIC

General public is individuals, citizen action groups, consumer bodies, the media, the government and so forth that can affect an entrepreneur's ability to run his or her enterprise. Surely you have heard or watch on the news about stop the oil, extinction rebellion, anti capitalist, anti war, anti fur, anti animal testing, black lives matters protests and so forth, all these do cause interruption to business activities and times force enterprise's to cease altogether.

General public considerations

Imagine, how many people including yourself, would like to live next to a power station, a quarry, a night club and so forth. In many places there exists residential, commercial, and industrial areas, factors like, noise, dust, smoke, traffic, and so forth have to be taken into account, this general public consideration. General public allows each and every enterprise to operate.

General public actions

Example 1: The government

In 2006 Swedish retailer IKEA was planning to expand significantly in the UK, opening a string of stores in city centres. It wanted to spend £1bn (1.4bn Euros) on 10 new stores as part of a revamped strategy, seeing it shift its focus away from new out-of-town sites, its efforts were thwarted by **local planning restrictions**, comes 2021, with most city centres becoming ghost towns, the power has shifted, IKEA bought former Topshop Oxford circus flagship store to convert it into a city-centre shop.

Example 2: Consumer bodies

In 2005 Citizen advice a charitable organization issued a super-complaint (defined by section 11(1) of the Enterprise Act 2002 (EA02) as a complaint submitted by a designated consumer body 'any feature', or a combination of features, of a market in the UK for goods or services is or appears to be significantly harming the interests of consumers') to the Office of Fair of Trading (OFT) about miss-sold Personal Protection Insurance (PPI) which was eventually ruled in consumers' favour that ended in banks paying back over £40 billion pounds in compensation.

There countless other groups whose individual or collective actions can impact an enterprise's in one way or another

PART III:

An entrepreneur in the long term

GENERAL ECONOMIC CONDITIONS

What has general economic conditions to do with?

General economic conditions have to do with income of an entire country. General economic conditions cover growth, trade agreements, currency, interest rates, taxation, inflation, wages, low unemployment, sector and labour availability. Changing economic conditions present both opportunities and threats.

Growth

Growth can come from domestic consumption, public spending, net exports, that is exports minus imports. Growth does encourage spending and subsequently increase the circulation of money in an economy. The UK is domestic consumption-led, it relies heavily on households spending for its economic growth. The opposite of growth is recession.

Currency

Most exports and imports transactions involve currency exchange. The problem is the bulk of major currencies use floating model, the leading currencies in global markets is the US dollar followed by the Euro, then Chinese Yuan, Japanese Yen and so forth. Due to global supplies, currency fluctuations affect every enterprise indiscriminately. Fluctuating currencies can wipe out a large chunk of profit if an enterprise exports and imports large amounts of products under different currency denominations. If a currency depreciates too much against the leading currencies, it does considerably reduce the purchasing power in global markets.

Consequences of currency depreciation

Example: Airbus

Suppliers' payments	Customers' payments
Euro zone – Euros € Great Britain – British pounds £ International – US dollars $	International - US dollars $

In 2009 the weak US currency wiped €1 billion ($1.46 billion) off AIRBUS revenues, as the dollar depreciated 10% against the Euro, after this incident Airbus decided to pay all its European suppliers in US dollars instead of Euros.

International trade

International trade is to imports and exports.

Imports	Exports
Imports measure the value of products and services that enter the domestic territory of a country irrespective of their final destination.	Exports measure the value of products and services which leave the domestic territory of a country, irrespective of whether they have been processed in the domestic territory or not.

Trade deficits vs. surpluses

Trade deficit between one country and another trading partner country happens when that country imports more that it exports to a partner, that is, negative net exports and the other way around, trade surplus happens when a country exports more to the partner than it imports, positive net exports.

Importance of International trade

In all developed economies, international trade represents a significant share of gross domestic product (GDP). International trade is a major source of economic revenue for any nation that is considered a world power. Without international trade, nations would be limited to products produced and services provided within their own borders, that is, the internal market.

Trade agreements

There exist bilateral trade agreements among nations that have reduced obstacles to trade this is globalization. Example EU single market, COMESA, ECOWAS, NAFTA, ASEAN and so forth.

Economic globalization

A core element of globalization is the expansion of international trade through the elimination or reduction of trade barriers, such as import tariffs, that is, taxes or duties imposed for influence or domestic markets protection, movement of capital, products, services, people as in labour and knowledge. Economic globalization is irreversible.

Economic globalization enablers

Economic globalization would not have materialized if it was not for multinational corporations, large size enterprises operating in several countries and conglomerates, diversified large enterprises and international transactions, think of the world without Coca Cola, McDonalds' KFC's, Boeing, Rolls Royce, GE, Siemens, Mastercard or Visa!

Proximity and trade

Despite globalization, most trade still happens between a host country and other neighbouring countries, that is countries in close geographic proximity this is due to **logistical (movement of products and services)** and **geopolitical (international relations as influenced by geography)** considerations. Over 40% of UK exports go to the EU.

Inflation and wages

Inflation has to do with price rises over a period. Unless wages which is the main source of income for most households rises, inflation reduces the purchasing power. When inflation bites, essential products and services hold-up, the non-essential counterparts get clobbered, in other words, sales of non-essential do decline sharply. The opposite of inflation is deflation.

High wages economy fallacies

Higher wages are just a number, a pipe dream unless they are linked to households rising cost of living - rising level of prices relating to a range of everyday basic goods, like, food, rent/mortgages, healthcare, utilities and so forth, and periodically not annually adjusted. You would rather have a low wage economy with low cost of living that the higher wages outstripped by the cost of living.

Low unemployment

When a country is close to full employment, it can create a problem in some sectors, making it difficult to attract workers. There is a shortage of agricultural workers, construction, elderly care you name it across the UK.

Sector and labour availability

Every country's economy has primary, secondary and tertiary sectors of industry in different percentages. For the advanced economies the largest sector by employment is tertiary, followed by highly mechanized and automated secondary and a tiny primary. Meaning, there are more people available for tertiary sector jobs than secondary and primary in that order.

Interest rates

Almost every enterprise use borrowing in some form, interest is paid from profit earned, depending on the level of borrowing, interest rate rises can wipe out all the profit, prevent an enterprise from securing more credit or loans and ultimately lead to total collapse.

Taxation

Apart from Value Added Tax, Stamp duty, and so forth that are paid on products or services sold to the last customer, other taxes are paid from profit. Taxation like interest rates can increase and decrease costs, rises in income, corporation, dividend, savings tax, national insurance contributions can deter investments and employing people.

Sector, division and activities

Sector of industry	Division of industry	Activities
Primary	Agriculture, forestry and fishing	Changing process of natural resources into primary products
	Mining and quarrying	
Secondary	Manufacturing	Production, demolition and erection of structures using primary products
	Construction	
Tertiary	Electricity, gas, steam and air conditioning	Provision of non product equivalents (services) to enterprises and consumers
	Water, sewerage, waste & remediation	
	Wholesale and retail trade	
	Motor vehicles and motorcycles repair	
	Transportation and storage	
	Accommodation and food service	
	Information and communication	
	Financial and insurance	
	Real estate	
	Professional, scientific and technical	
	Administrative and support service	
	Public administration and defence	
	Compulsory social security	
	Education	
	Health and social work	
	Arts, entertainment and recreation	
	Other services	

SOCIAL, CULTURAL AND DEMOGRAPHIC CONDITIONS

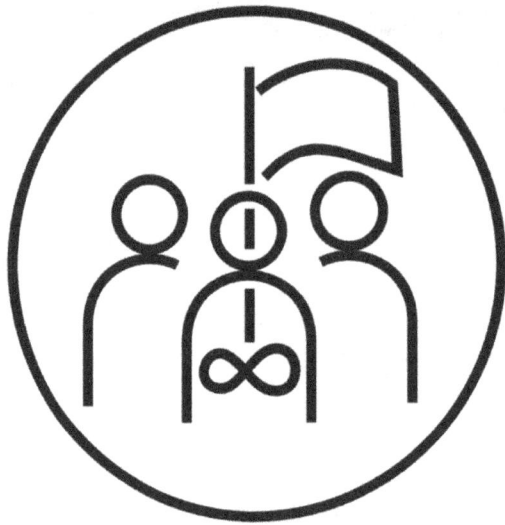

What have social, cultural, and demographic conditions to do with?

Social, cultural, and demographic conditions have to do with people in an entire country. Changing social, cultural, and demographic conditions present both opportunities and threats.

Social conditions

Social conditions have to do with people in general living together in an organized and harmonious way, social conditions cover education, health, housing, crime, mass media, women, and minorities.

Education

Education is to skills. The main issue is skills shortage. Poor education system equals skills shortages due to mismatch and under skilling, a threat if your enterprise is looking for highly-skilled people. Rapid changes in technology do contribute to skills shortages as everyone is playing a catch up. For example, with electric cars, there is not enough mechanics trained to maintain and service them, with green energy, there is a shortage of engineers to install wind turbines, heat pumps, solar panels, and so forth. There also exist skills shortages where employers are asking for too many skills from jobseekers.

Health

Humans can function normally only if they are of sound mind in a sound body. Millions of days and billions of pounds are lost every year due to ill health, a cost to the whole country indiscriminately.

Housing

As an entrepreneur you are not concerned with housing per se but the costs of buying, leasing, or renting, commercial, industrial or residential. The government approach is on having mixed income housing that broadly encompasses many types of dwellings such as apartments, town homes, and/or single-family homes for a people with a range of income levels. There reality is, high rents and unsuitable accommodation do drive a particular workforce, demographic you name it out of places, a threat if your enterprise depends on onsite workforce and a particular demographic and opportunity if you are a developer. The economy needs all kinds of workers waste collectors, the nurses, and the cleaners whose shoulders are supporting the apex of the pyramid. Business rents tend to be per square metre the closer to places with higher footfall the higher the rent per square metre.

Crime

As entrepreneur you are not concerned with crime per se but costs. Crimes add costs indiscriminately. There are many types of crimes, to name but a few, cyber, shoplifting, thefts, piracy, bootlegging, copyright infringements, you name it. There is a say, there is no crime without opportunity, as an entrepreneur you can minimize the opportunities using appropriate measures.

Mass media

The purpose of mass media is to educate, entertain and inform the public. Mass media has massive influence on people, problem is, the bulk of mass media content has little educational or entertainment value these days, there is too much misinformation that negatively impact the ability of people to live together in harmony.

Women and minorities

As entrepreneur you are not concerned with women and minorities per se but equal opportunities. Women and minorities make more than half of populations in many countries across the world, yet they face discrimination, you will be missing out if you don't tap into women and minorities and on top of this depending on enterprise size, there are gender pay gap reporting, equal opportunities policies that have to be implemented if you employ people.

Cultural conditions

Cultural conditions have to do with consumption, that is, the use of products or services. There are products and services that are mainstream and others that are fringe, culture specific. We live in multicultural society. Customers and employees do come from all walks of life and different cultural backgrounds. One must appreciate cultural differences.

Demographic conditions

Demographic conditions have to do with most demand and workforce availability, demographic conditions cover births, deaths, geographic population density, immigration, emigration.
There is higher population density in places with most resources, births and deaths balance each other, dependency ratio, there must be more economically active people at work than the non active, namely children and the retired elderly, immigration and emigration balance each other, where emigration does contribute to exodus of talent, immigration does the opposite, brain drain from poorer countries, which is somewhat unethical poaching people from places where they are needed most.

UK demography

Around 84% of UK population live in England	Around 82% of England population live in the Midlands, East Anglia and the South.

It is evident, the most demand is where the 82% of population lives, the reason why you have north-south divide, many enterprise chose to set up in the south.

NATURAL CONDITIONS

What have natural conditions to do with?

Natural conditions have to do with the surface of the earth that supports life and infrastructure, namely, utilities, telecommunications, roads, ports, railways, airports, schools, hospitals and so forth without which no business activities can take place in an entire country. As far as an enterprise is concerned the most important issue is sustainability, creating an enterprise that fulfils the wants of today without compromising the wants of the future. Changing natural conditions present both opportunities and threats to running a sustainable business. The following are key natural conditions issues, a country's existing infrastructure, global oil and energy demand, fresh water consumption, global food demand, side effects of economic activities, environmental taxes and so forth.

Current UK infrastructure

Not enough schools, hospitals, roads, ports, airports, pipelines, telecommunication lines, power-lines and so forth are being built to meet demand. The UK has crumbling schools and hospitals, potholed and congested roads, probably the most inefficient but expensive railway on the planet, rusted Victorian water pipes, inadequate water reservoirs, poor drainage and sewerage system, slow and intermittent broadband, and so many other problems that add to delays and costs.

Global oil demand

Over 60% of oil is used in transportation. Demand often does outstrip supply. There is a tendency of biggest oil producing countries to cap production to maintain price and generate more profit. Although, there is a growing trend towards hybrid battery powered transportation this is simply shifting the problem to more energy consumption. The point is, rising oil prices is a windfall to related enterprises and additional costs to all the others. For heavy oil and derivatives consuming enterprise, rising prices at the pumps and elsewhere, can cripple and times bankrupt you.

Global energy demand

Without energy modern life will cease to exist. Energy comes from renewable and non-renewable sources. Demand often does outstrip supply. The bulk of energy is still coming from non-renewable sources, moving away from non-renewable sources will take a long time as to integrate renewable sources into the existing non-renewable infrastructure requires big investment. The point to remember is, rising energy prices is a windfall to related enterprises and additional costs to all the others. For heavy energy using enterprise, rising bills can wipe all the profit and at times closure of an enterprise operations.

Fresh water consumption

Agriculture by far uses the most clean fresh water, believe it or not, Artificial intelligence (AI) is fresh clean water thirsty too, it consumes a lot in cooling and powering data-centres.

Supporting life

No human can survive without food, water, healthcare, air, shelter, or clothing. With ballooning global population and dwindling resources, it is become harder and harder to meet these demands.

Global food demand

Global food demand increases with global growing population. The bulk of food production requires land not pots and containers. The key issues are productivity, adaptability due to climate change and emissions. Food is essential, due to global food demand and lower supply, there is a hike in prices across the board and where people have to spend a big chunk of incomes on food, there is reduction in spending elsewhere. When shortages persist, some foods are taken off menus completely. In 2023 Macdonald's and Burger King removed them tomatoes from the menus in India due to sharp rise in price due to shortages

World without energy!

Energy is the basis of industrial and tertiary civilizations, energy drives modern economies. **Without energy**, modern life will cease to exist, humans will go back to living primitive hunter-gatherer, hunting and foraging lives!

Side effects of economic activities

The main contributor to pollution to land, air and water are human activities. The world is running out of landfill space, there is air pollution everywhere, plastic, clothing, white goods rubbish is scattered along every corner of the planet. Air pollution and climate change are two sides of the same coin. Air pollution is the main contributor to climate change. Non renewable sources of energy namely coal, oil and gas alone account for over three quarters of global greenhouse gas emissions and nearly nine tenths of all carbon dioxide emissions.

Environmental taxes

We are all paying for the unintended consequences of damage to the environment in environmental taxes, there are congestion charges, CO2 based car tax bands, air passenger duty, landfill taxes to name but a few, all these are costs.

TECHNOLOGICAL CONDITIONS

What have technological conditions to do with?

Technological conditions have to do with off the shelf or custom made, proprietary or open technology that is available for enterprises' practical uses within a country. The use of fire is the most important early humankind invention, technological advances like fire, ignite innovation. Changing technological conditions present both opportunities and threats. The most important technological conditions for an entrepreneur to be aware of are the technology lifecycles and dominant designs.

What are technology life cycles?

Technology life cycles covers every stage of a product, from concept prototype through to final product and ultimately obsolescence, the end where the product is not used as much to justify investment in producing any more. Technology life cycle can be measured in months, years, decades, centuries and so on. The best thing about technology lifecycles is that, it is not abrupt but tends to follow a predictable pattern and allow time to get ready for a switchover.

Example - Mobile phone technology

Mobile phones are built to work on specific types of allocated frequencies.

- 2G technology was suitable for making calls and sending text messages.
- 3G suitable for making calls and sending text messages and possible to access the internet more effectively through mobile phones.
- 4G suitable for making calls and sending text messages makes it easier to access the internet on your mobile, tablet or laptop, ideal for services that demand more capacity, like video streaming, mapping, and social networking sites on the move.
- 5G is the new generation of wireless technology.

Most mobile providers have switched off 2G and are or will be switching off 3G in a near future, you cannot keep hold of your Nokia 1100 or 1110 as they will not work due to being incompatible with current frequencies. There are so many examples of obsolete technologies like Floppy diskettes, VHS tapes, disposable cameras and so forth, they are not useless just no longer used by many and thus not worth producing them anymore.

What is a dominant design?

Dominant design is a standard widely adopted design wide usage not superiority. There exist many dominant open and proprietary standard designs, to name but a few, all electrical distribution is Alternating current AC between 110, 240, 415 Volts in 50 hertz, the car manual and automatic gears, Schrader (American) pneumatic tyre valve, generators and motors, and so many others follow the same principles regardless of manufacturers, computer hardware uses the same components namely resistors, capacitors, transformers, diodes as standalone or on integrated circuits, Google android and Apple IOS are dominant cellular phone operating systems, Google play and Apple app store are dominant mobile app platforms. The point is, regardless of an enterprise's size, it is futile to try to compete against a dominant design.

Examples of dominant designs

Automatic gearbox

All automatic cars have no clutch, gears shift automatically, all the driver has to is, to move the gear to the right position as indicated. The configuration follows the same hydraulic transmission principle invented by Brazilian engineers Fernando Lehly Lemos and José Braz Araripe and developed by General motors in the 1930s and 40s regardless of car brand.

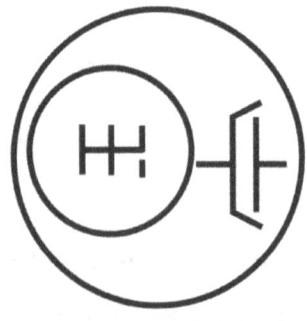

Manual gearbox

All manual cars use a clutch to shift through the gears. The configuration follows the same principle invented by Frenchmen Rene Panhard and Emile Levassor in the 1890s regardless of car brand.

Electricity – Direct current (DC)

All dry cell batteries in small appliances – phones, torches, radios use Thomas Edison's 1880s direct current invention.

Electricity - Alternating current (AC)

All generators, motors, transformers, electricity transmission uses Serbian American Nikola Tesla's 1880s alternating current invention.

POLITICAL AND LEGAL CONDITIONS

What have political and legal conditions to do with?

A country's political stability and legal system are essential for domestic - from own country, foreign direct – from third country with full ownership, foreign portfolio - from third country with partial ownership investments. Changing political and legal conditions present both opportunities and threats.

Political decisions

In a free enterprise system, enterprises are self-regulating; the role of the government is to create conditions to which enterprises can thrive not to lecture them what to do. In any country, if an incoming or existing government prioritizes economy over politics, there is stability in the markets, vice versa, if an incoming or existing government prioritizes politics over economy, there is turmoil in the markets with added costs.

Political decisions and their impacts

Example 1

Brexit 2016
Brexit, holding a referendum to leave the EU made no economic sense, the government of the day prioritized politics over economy, the consequences of which are, erection of barriers to trade with the biggest trading bloc on the planet that has shrunk the UK economy, added unnecessary costs in administration and tariffs and since the freedom of movement ended with it, the country has experienced skills shortage in every sector of industry!

Example 2:

Big bang
In 1986 London Stock exchange was deregulated, London became global financial hub transacting trillions of dollars daily.

The legal system

Legal system is to the rule of law, the principle that, no one is above the law. There are laws governing the running of enterprises, to name but a few, sales of goods act, provision of services act, rights of third parties, credit terms, statutory rights, warranties, guarantees, distance selling, cooling off period, age of majority, that is, the lowest age of legal adulthood, mergers and acquisitions, intellectual property, namely, patents, registered designs, copyrights, trademarks, data protection, planning laws, environmental laws, trade unions, antitrust laws, immigration laws, and so forth.

Intellectual property

Intellectual property is about protecting your creations from infringements. Intellectual property is a valuable non-physical asset. Owners of intellectual property can live off their protected work through licensing, royalties and so forth, for years and at times for life.

Selling and buying

All selling and buying involves exchange of contract between a seller and a buyer, for most part, only people of sound mind and above legal age can enter a contract placing legal responsibility to both parties.

Term, condition, warranty

A term is a word or phrase that forms part of a contract. A condition is the main term of a contract, the breach of which gives the right to terminate a contract. A warranty is a lesser term of condition the breach of which does not give a right to terminate a contract but does give the right to claim damages. For customers, a guarantee and warranty are the same. A contract can be in written or unwritten format.

Let the seller beware

Let the seller beware principle places the responsibility to ensure a product on offer is of saleable quality to the seller. Buyers can claim remedies like refunds or replacement from the seller if expected quality is not met. Most enterprises sell products under let the seller beware principle.

Let the buyer beware

Let the buyer beware principle places the responsibility to ensure the product on offer is of buyable quality to the buyer. Buyers cannot claim remedies like refunds or replacement from the seller if expected quality is not met. Auctions, education, third party disclaimers are examples.

Reasonable skill and care

Service is not a physical product and thus impossible to universally judge saleable quality. It is a matter of interpretation between the contracting parties to agree what is deemed reasonable skill and care. Buyers can claim remedies like refunds or rectification if expected reasonable skill and care test is not met by the seller.

Service level agreement (SLA)

Service level agreement is a contractual agreement between a service provider and recipient of the minimum standard the service provider is required to meet.

Standard contracts

Just like writing specifications, drawing a contract for every selling and buying is time consuming and costly hence the use of standard contracts. Standard contracts are on take it or leave it terms that are rarely read. Regardless of whether the contract is read or not as a seller you must have a written contract where you clearly express your terms, conditions and warranties bearing in mind varied legal jurisdictions, that is, the boundaries to which a particular law applies.

Ignorance of the law does not excuse

Ignorance of the law does not excuse is a legal principle holding that you cannot get away from breaking the law on grounds that you were unaware it existed, it is everyone responsibility to understand the applicable laws. As an entrepreneur, you must follow the law, onset and continuously monitor for any changes in timely manner and implement them as they happen.

Intellectual property infringement - Napster story

Napster pioneered and paved the way to downloads and streaming we have today. It all started in 1999 when a Northeastern University dropout named Shawn Fanning created Napster (his nickname at university) as a peer to peer file sharing music download service that at one point swelled to more than 70 million users. It was the disrupting force that brought to the world the appetite for free music downloads and contributed immensely to the fall of singles sales. The downfall of Napster was contributed by the naivety of the founder, who did not understand copyright laws. After lawsuits by AOL Time Warner, EMI, Bertelsmann among a few and the injunctions from US appeals court that forced it to remain shut in 2001 as a result it lost the bulk of the users, by the time it was bought by Melody VR for £53 million in 2020 it had around 3 million users. If it wasn't for copyright infringement Napster would have been the Google of downloads and streaming today.

Patent expiry

A patent as protected intellectual property has a finite lifespan. Once a patent has expired anyone can copy and use it. Patent expiry is a competitive advantage loss to the owner but an opportunity to many others that can capitalize on costs of production, where all you need to do is find the ingredients and put them together without spending a penny on research and development. In pharmaceutical industry patent expiry leads production of generic medicines that are way far cheaper than branded. Patent expiry change proprietary to open to all.

THE END

www.ingramcontent.com/pod-product-compliance
Lightning Source LLC
Chambersburg PA
CBHW081849170526
45167CB00007B/2945